# UNDISCOVERED
# Museums
## of
# London

**Eloise Danto**

**SURREY BOOKS**
230 East Ohio Street
Suite 120
Chicago, Illinois 60611

**UNDISCOVERED MUSEUMS OF LONDON** is published by
Surrey Books, 230 E. Ohio St., Suite 120, Chicago, Illinois 60611.
Phone: (312) 751-7330.

This book is manufactured in the United States of America.

Second edition. 1 2 3 4 5

**Library of Congress Cataloging-in-Publication Data**

Danto, Eloise.
    Undiscovered Museums of London / Eloise Danto. — 2nd ed.
    138 p.    cm.
    Rev. ed. of: Museums of London. 1989.
    Includes index.
    ISBN 0-940625-35-0 : $8.95
    1. Museums—England—London—Guide-books. 2. London
(England)—Description—1981- —Guide-books. I. Danto, Eloise.
Museums of London. II. Title.
AM43.L6D35 1991                90-24481
069'.09421'2—dc20              CIP

**Illustrations and maps by Eloise Danto.**
Editorial Production: Bookcrafters, Inc., Chicago.
Cover Design: Hughes & Co., Chicago.
Typesetting: On Track Graphics, Inc., Chicago.

Single copies of this book may be ordered by sending check or
money order for $10.95 (includes postage and handling) per book to
Surrey Books at the above address.

The "Undiscovered Museums" series is distributed to the trade by
Publishers Group West.

**Cover Photos** *(clockwise):*
Gloster Gladiator, Battle of Britain
  Museum in Royal Air Force Museum.
Furnishings exhibit, Design Museum.
The Palm House, Royal Botanic (Kew)
  Gardens.

**Other Books in This Series:**
Undiscovered Museums of Florence
Undiscovered Museums of New York
Undiscovered Museums of Paris

The imposing British Museum.
*All photos courtesy of the British
  Tourist Authority.*

# CONTENTS AND INDEX

# INTRODUCTION

London is one of the great Meccas of Western secular culture. Like Florence, Paris, Rome, and New York, it draws us in. At least one pilgrimage must be arranged, and preferably several in the course of a lifetime. High on the list of shrines to be visited are London's repository temples of culture, its museums. In this book you will find not only the large, prestigious institutions known the world over but also the smaller, equally interesting but largely "undiscovered" museums of London.

London's museums are many and various. They offer something for everyone no matter what your particular interest might be. For example, London has more military museums than any other city—eight, to be exact. It has six science museums, four children's museums, nine fine arts museums, and six other categories of museum, including individual homes such as those of Sigmund Freud and William Hogarth. London has a small museum devoted entirely to the history of the fan—and the world's ultimate museum in both size and scope: the British Museum. Since some visitors prefer certain types or categories of museums, I have included a "category" index at the back of this book. Thus, if you are seeking an historic museum, simply look under that listing. The "Contents" in the front of the book serves as a general index.

Not surprisingly, London is paradise for students and advocates of the sciences, the humanities, architecture, politics, and theater. What may be surprising is the fascination London holds for lovers of art history and what can be called the art traveler. If asked to name the art capital of the West, you might say Rome or Paris. But London, too, has great artistic riches. In addition to the museums already mentioned, the city has nearly forty temples of art of various sorts, not counting gardens, workshops, or studios of illustrious artists, dead and alive: for example, the William Morris Gallery and the Queen's Gallery in Buckingham Palace. Since language plays little or no role in the enjoyment and appreciation of art, you can experience these fascinating riches whatever your native tongue may be.

The museums of London, including its art museums, are of course enriched by their setting, most noticeably, perhaps, by the historical and architectural surroundings. Few cities in Europe can match London for its wealth of historical remains and ruins. Not only is the city filled with buildings of incalculable historic and artistic value but a sharp eye might discover a fragment of ancient history lying unnoticed along a city block.

Indeed, London is steeped in history. Today's city is only the uppermost layer of a veritable layer cake. During the 1950s, for example, substantial remains of a pagan Roman temple (A.D. 43) were unearthed, confirming that the Roman city of Londinium lies beneath the London we now see. Londinium developed into an important administrative center for the Roman Empire and lasted until the fifth century. But Londinium was not the first settlement located here. Archaeological findings indicate a Celtic occupation that lasted into the fifth century B.C. Other groups followed the Celts, each building over the ruins of its predecessors. Thus, there are several ancient cities beneath current London. You will see this succession in the Museum of London.

London's architectural personality also enhances the art traveler's enjoyment, thanks to the talents of several innovative, illustrious architects. Foremost among them in his own time, and still today, is Sir Christopher Wren, who rebuilt London after its disastrous fire of 1666. His credits include St. Paul's, Kensington Palace, Hampton

Court Palace, and more than fifty of London's churches. In the early 1600s, master designer Inigo Jones created Covent Garden and the Queen's House in Greenwich. John Nash in the late 1700s developed London's Regency style with his Marble Arch, Regent Street, and Buckingham Palace. Each and every one of these geniuses contributed to London's outstanding architectural heritage.

Now to practical matters.

Most of London's museums are open daily except for Mondays and major holidays. On those days you can visit a castle, a zoo, or a cathedral. Or there's always Madame Tussaud's or the Planetarium. A few museums, however, are open for just a few hours a day or only one or two days a week. Be sure to check the schedules before beginning your museum trek. I have provided each museum's opening times and days at the beginning of its section.

More than half of London's museums allow free admission, and several of the rest have only a suggested donation. For those with admission fees, almost all offer a discount to seniors and a special rate for families, so take notice of the possibilities when paying your entry fee. I have quoted each museum's adult entry fee only, at the beginning of each section.

It is becoming more convenient for museum-goers to have their meals within museums. Museums have redesigned their cafeterias, museum food has improved in style, and prices are often lower than at outside restaurants. Thus the museum gains additional income, and the visitor is comfortably accommodated. The Tate, the National Army Museum, the Royal Academy, and the British Museum are a few examples of London's better museum restaurants, successfully attracting their visitors to "dine at the time."

In keeping with London's reputation as one of the world's great centers for the performing arts, its museums more and more frequently host scheduled entertainment and educational programs in dance, theater, poetry, and music. Call your favorite museum for a schedule of events. You don't want to miss out on a special performance that might be there for only a day or two during your stay.

Gift shops play a significant role in the appeal of their museums. The visitor usually gravitates to the museum shop, which often specializes in items and gifts directly related to the collections. For example, the range of books about gardens and gardening and other items of horticultural interest offered at the Botanic Gardens' shop is unmatched. The same could be said for the Museum of the Moving Image, in which the store's offering of unique show biz treats is mind boggling. Be sure to buy your gift when and where you see it. Chances are it will not be found in the next museum.

Unless you prefer to cross London on foot, the wisest way to get from one museum to another is by way of the Underground, or Tube. Each section in this book lists both the station nearest the museum in question and the line or lines taken to reach it. Ten separate Underground lines traverse London, converging at several transfer points. Thus, your museum travels become fairly simple. In cases where a museum cannot be reached by Tube, I have suggested using the Light Railway (quicker) or the River Boat along the Thames (more aesthetic).

I hope that you, the culture-oriented traveler, will not only enjoy the recognizably popular museums but be enticed into visiting some of London's lesser-known "undiscovered" museums. These museums can be intimate and revealing. They offer insight into their collections. Their staffs are available for information and anecdotes. Each museum has its own story and its own personality. The Shakespeare Globe Museum, Dickens House, and the Museum of Garden History are three examples of the pleasures of small museums.

All of London's museums are located near one or more of the nearly 800 acres of parkland in central London. Avail yourself of this treat either before or after your museum visit. It's a pause that will more than refresh. Besides, it is essential that you avoid the familiar museum-goer's pitfall—too many museums and too much information in too little time. Take it slowly and plan one step at a time. Do not attempt a museum marathon—it's sure disaster.

Always keep your London maps in hand. I strongly recommend three helpful guides: PENGUIN LONDON MAPGUIDE, a small 50-page paper booklet, $5, bought in the U.S., Canada, or London, in which London is broken down into easy-to-reach and easy-to-understand segments. Another indispensable helper is a fold-out map called BRITAIN LONDON MAP, bought at newsstands in London and elsewhere in the U.K. and at the British Tourist Authority. Cost is $1. Combine these with a copy of LONDON CONNECTIONS, obtainable free at Information Centres in major train stations and airports in London. This is an excellent fold-out diagram of London's Underground, bus, and rail systems.

Now that you have armed yourself with information, insight, and aids of all sorts—including this guidebook and plenty of energy—I invite you to join me on an unusual journey. Come and explore London's treasure houses, magical museums, and palaces of culture. I promise you an extraordinary adventure and an unforgettable glimpse into London's illustrious past, present, and future.

## APSLEY HOUSE (Wellington Museum)

| | | | |
|---|---|---|---|
| **Open:** | Tues.-Sat. 11-5 | **Type:** | Military |
| **Closed:** | Mon., Major Holidays | **Address:** | 149 Piccadilly, Hyde Park Corner, WIV 9FA |
| **Tube:** | Hyde Park Corner (Piccadilly Line) | **Tel:** | 071-499-5676 |
| **Entry:** | £1.50 | | |

Apsley House is aptly called "Number One, London," after the illustrious First Duke of Wellington, né Arthur Wellesley (1769–1852), the swashbuckling military hero whose most famous portrait, painted by Lawrence, graces the wall of the Striped Room upstairs. This was his home from 1817 until his death. Not only was the Iron Duke one of England's greatest generals, defeating Napoleon at Waterloo and winning countless other victories, but he was Prime Minister from 1828 until 1830. The Duke collected fine art. His

Spanish paintings, unequalled in London, are here along with his fine portrait collection and military memorabilia, trophies, and honors. The grandest room is the 90-foot-long banquet room called the Waterloo Gallery. And that larger-than-life marble statue in the entry is none other than Napoleon Bonaparte, *sans* uniform.

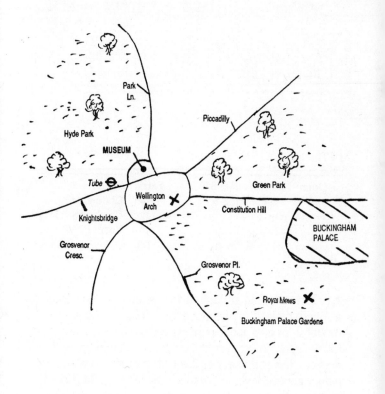

## BETHNAL GREEN MUSEUM OF CHILDHOOD

| | | | |
|---|---|---|---|
| **Open:** | Mon.-Thurs., Sat. 10-6; Sun. 2-6 | **Entry:** | Free |
| **Closed:** | Fri., Major Holidays | **Type:** | Children's |
| | | **Address:** | Cambridge Heath Road, E2 9PA |
| **Tube:** | Bethnal Green (Central Line) | **Tel:** | 071-980-3204 |

A branch of the Victoria & Albert, Bethnal Green contains a superb collection of antique toys, dolls, dollhouses, model ships and boats, puppets and marionettes, and a toy theater. Almost everything here is for children, with items dating as far back as the 17th century. Toys and games are everywhere, for this is the largest collection of childhood antiquities in the world, and simply charming. The second floor has a display of the social history of childhood, an antique wedding gown collection, antique children's clothing, antique nursery furniture, and a priceless collection of Teddy bears. The 100-year-old museum building is the original iron structure of the Victoria & Albert. Saturdays, special Play Days, and school holidays are set aside for open workshops and activities, when children are invited to participate in joyous play. Here's one of London's family favorites.

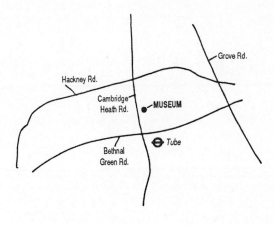

## BRITISH LIBRARY

| | | | |
|---|---|---|---|
| **Open:** | Mon.-Sat. 10-5; Sun. 2:30-6 | **Entry:** | Free |
| **Closed:** | Major Holidays | **Type:** | General |
| **Tube:** | Tottenham Court Road (Central, Northern Line) | **Address:** | Great Russell Street, WC1B 3D |
| | | **Tel:** | 071-636-1544 |

This temple of apparently limitless knowledge is only one branch of the British Library's 18. Housed in the east wing of the British Museum building, it possesses a vast, almost mind-boggling collection of books, including the famous Gutenberg Bible, and information. The Great Reading Room, with its spectacular dome, is open for serious scholars doing particular research on collections not available elsewhere. It is open to the public for a five-minute glimpse every hour on the hour. Happily, this circular room will remain with the Museum after the

Library moves to its own home (St. Pancras) in 1996. The new Library, 20 times the size of the present one, will be the world's largest research and reference center for humanities and sciences and will accommodate even more than the half-million researchers it now sees yearly.

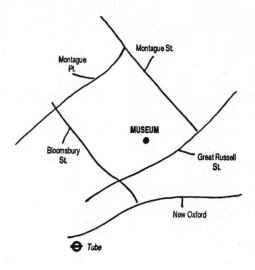

## BRITISH MUSEUM

| | | | |
|---|---|---|---|
| **Open:** | Mon.-Sat. 10-5; Sun. 2:30-6 | **Entry:** | Free |
| **Closed:** | Major Holidays | **Type:** | General |
| **Tube:** | Tottenham Court Road (Central, Northern Line) | **Address:** | Great Russell St., WC1B 3DG |
| | | **Tel:** | 071-636-1555 |

It would be hard to imagine a more quintessentially British museum than this one, which opened its doors in 1753. It's certainly one of London's most celebrated and magnificent museums, holding the world's largest and richest collection of antiquities. Do not attempt this museum without a floor plan, a huge block of time, and a well-thought-out plan of attack. It's ponderous in size. Illuminating displays cover from prehistoric times, through the Classic and Medieval eras, the Renaissance, and up to the present century. To make the collections more manageable for visitors, the museum is broken down into nine separate entities, so select your favorite subject upon entering. The writer has only high praise for the style of presentation, the excellent lighting, and the superb sense of order. Stately is the word. The Elgin Marbles are a must. And the Gift Shop, with its replicas of famous artifacts, can't be beat.

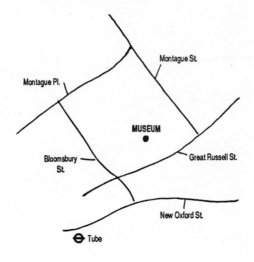

## CABINET WAR ROOMS

| | | | |
|---|---|---|---|
| **Open:** | Daily 10-6 | **Type:** | Military |
| **Closed:** | Major Holidays | **Address:** | Clive Steps, King |
| **Tube:** | Westminster | | Charles St., |
| | (Jubilee, Bakerloo | | SW1A 2A |
| | Line) | **Tel:** | 071-930-6961 |
| **Entry:** | £2.50 | | |

When Winston Churchill became prime minister in 1940, he took his cabinet and chiefs of staff and disappeared into the Cabinet War Rooms deep beneath London. In this underground bunker of 21 rooms he waged and won his war. His famous radio broadcasts were made here, still heard as you explore where he slept, ate, lived, and worked during the Blitz. His major decisions were made from the Map Room, where a 24-hour watch was maintained. The Cabinet Room was where England's top war strategists assembled in tense conferences. Maps and charts still line the walls, equipment remains, voice recordings are played. Each room is filled with crises. The atmosphere is electric with excitement. For a sense of the desperate struggle for Britain's survival that was World War II, the War Rooms are unparalleled.

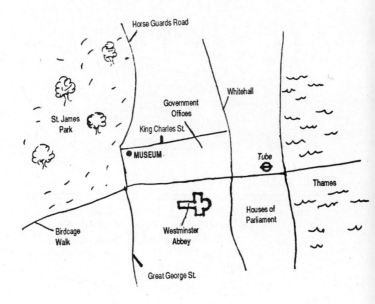

## COURTAULD INSTITUTE GALLERIES

| | | | |
|---|---|---|---|
| **Open:** | Mon.-Sat. 10-6;<br>Sun. 2-6; Tues.<br>till 8 | **Entry:**<br>**Type:**<br>**Address:** | £2.50<br>Fine Arts<br>Somerset House, |
| **Closed:** | Major Holidays | | Strand, WC2R |
| **Tube:** | Temple ( Circle/<br>District Line) | **Tel:** | ORN<br>071-873-2526 |

Somerset House, which houses these Galleries, is a masterpiece of Georgian classical architecture built to house government offices in the late 1700s. In fact, the Strand area was designed with an eye toward cultural perfection. The Galleries are a part of both the University of London and the Courtauld Institute, Britain's leading center for the study of art. The Galleries contain only the most magnificent French Impressionist and Post-Impressionist works. Samuel Courtauld, an impeccable collector, founded the Institute in 1931. Roger Fry, of the famed

Bloomsbury Group, bequeathed his collection of 20th-century works and West African sculptures. In fact, the Galleries' entire contents represent bequests of private individuals—astute collectors from the world over. All this plus furniture, textiles, tapestries, carpets, and decorative arts. Courtauld is distinguished and elegant. I guarantee you will spend many pleasurable hours here. Courtauld is sophisticated, simple, and perfect.

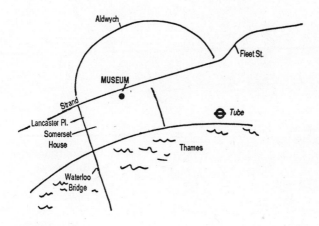

## COURT DRESS COLLECTION (Kensington Palace)

| | | | |
|---|---|---|---|
| **Open:** | Mon.-Sat. 9-5; Sun. 1-5 | **Entry:** | £1.50, combined with State Apartments |
| **Closed:** | Major Holidays | **Type:** | General |
| **Tube:** | High St., Kensington (Circle/District Line) | **Address:** | Kensington Palace, W8 4PX |
| | | **Tel:** | 071-937-9561 |

Since the Royal Family lives here, only a portion of the Palace is open to the public. Walk around to the back of the Palace, which faces Kensington Park. It's this corner of the Palace that houses the Court Dress Collection displayed in period room settings reflecting court etiquette, convention, ritual, and behavior during political and state occasions, drawing-room receptions, and important royal events. Elegant court dress and manners for ladies and gentlemen of this elite section of society are traced. Although court fashion has traditionally been out of step with high fashion, the entry of Her Royal Highness, Diana, the Princess of Wales, upon the scene has brought royal fashion to a new high level. As a finale, you see her elegant wedding gown. After your visit, stop in at the Orangerie Tea Room for your midday break, then take a stroll through Kensington Park.

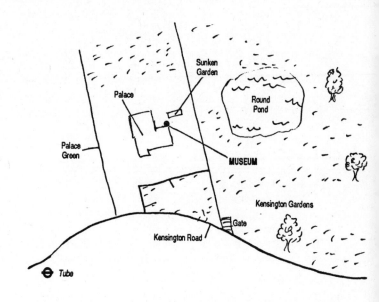

## CRICKET CLUB MUSEUM

| | | | |
|---|---|---|---|
| **Open:** | Mon.-Sat. 10:30-5 on Match Days during Cricket Season | **Entry:** | £2.00 |
| | | **Type:** | General |
| | | **Address:** | Lord's Ground, St. John's Wood, NW8 8QN |
| **Tube:** | St. John's Wood (Jubilee Line) | **Tel:** | 071-289-1611 |

Lord's, London's major cricket center, is aptly known as the "Mecca of Cricket." Lord's Ground is named after its founder, Sir Thomas Lord, who created this cherished playing field in 1814. It's the home and headquarters of the Marylebone Cricket Club and Cricket Council, which hosts international competitions for that most English of games, and whose 12 acres host matches and competitions April through September in an atmosphere of elegant, dignified sportsmanship. The museum building has a gallery containing paintings and photographs illustrating historical Cricketana from the 1600s and a library with a fine collection of cricket books and manuscripts plus an indoor cricket school. Cocktails in the Lounge Bar and picnics in the Coronation Garden, naturally. If you harbor nostalgia and affection for cricketers of all times and nationalities, Lord's should be visited, and please drop in at the Lord's Shop for Cricketanical Gifts.

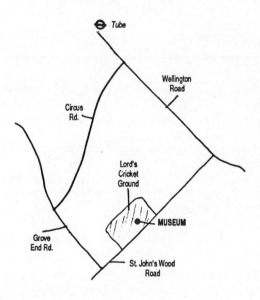

## DESIGN MUSEUM

| | | | |
|---|---|---|---|
| **Open:** | Tues.-Sun. 11:30-6:30 | **Entry:** | £1.00 |
| **Closed:** | Mondays, Major Holidays | **Type:** | Decorative Arts |
| **Tube:** | Tower Hill (Circle/District Line) | **Address:** | Butlers Wharf, 28 Shad Thames, LSE 2YD |
| | | **Tel:** | 071-403-6933 |

This is one of London's newest museums, created in 1989. It is large, bright, airy, and devoted to the best and the brightest in industrial design from furniture, clothing, electrical conveniences, automobiles, and typewriters to radio and everyday mass-produced goods and services and pleasure-seeking devices. The three-story building, a 1950s warehouse, contains the museum, a library, a theater, and the Blueprint Cafe overlooking the Thames. Temporary exhibitions and the permanent collection are imaginative. The Study

Collection shows hundreds of everyday objects in various stages of design and development. Here's a nicely done show with plenty of class. The museum runs a ferry service to and from the Tower Pier, unless you prefer walking across the Tower Bridge. The immediate neighborhood, called Docklands, is an example of London's successful efforts to break away from its traditional ambiance into a trendy, upbeat area with residences, theaters, and businesses.

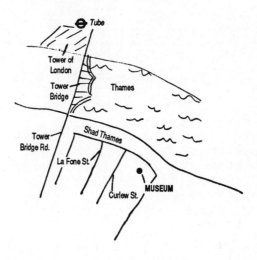

## DICKENS HOUSE MUSEUM

| | | | |
|---|---|---|---|
| **Open:** | Mon.-Sat. 10-5 | **Entry:** | £1.00 |
| **Closed:** | Sun., Major | **Type:** | Individual |
| | Holidays | **Address:** | 48, Doughty St., |
| **Tube:** | Russell Square | | WC1N 2LF |
| | (Piccadilly Line) | **Tel:** | 071-405-2127 |

This was the home of England's revered author Charles
Dickens from 1837 to 1839, during which time he
wrote *Oliver Twist, Nicholas Nickleby, The Pickwick
Papers,* and several other great books. He is still
immensely popular, judging from the local crowds at
the museum and the length of time they stay to study
and read. The four-story building, intimate and personal, is furnished as it was in Dickens' day, and it is
filled with personal family and friends' memorabilia,
drawings, manuscripts, and first editions. For a particularly pleasant sensation, linger in the upstairs Drawing

Room. Its ambiance lends to a sense of a small gathering of Dickens and friends sipping coffee, discussing current affairs and news of interest in the literary world. The museum is lovingly looked after by Mr. Parker and his staff. Do stop by the Museum Shop for your gifts and souvenirs.

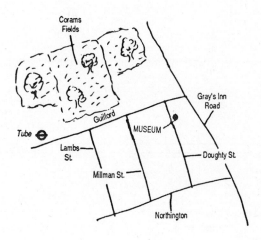

## DULWICH PICTURE GALLERY

| | | | |
|---|---|---|---|
| **Open:** | Tues.-Fri. 10-1, 2-5; Sat 11-5, Sun. 2-5 | **Entry:** | £1.00 |
| | | **Type:** | Fine Arts |
| | | **Address:** | College Road, SE21 7BG |
| **Closed:** | Mon., Public Holidays | **Tel:** | 081-693-5254 |
| **Tube:** | Dulwich BritRail, West | | |

The Gallery, originally conceived as and still considered the Perfect Building, was designed by Sir John Soane (see Sir John Soane's Museum) in 1817 and has been added onto and enhanced several times. It began in 1799 as the private collection of Noel Desenfans, who lies in the museum mausoleum opposite his wife. Each of the 12 salons in these stylish premises are enhanced by a fabulous collection of French and English furnishings, and they glow with natural light from immense skylights. Some of Europe's finest painters—Gainsborough, Van Dyck, Tiepolo, Reynolds, Rembrandt, and Velasquez, rarely seen outside Madrid—are displayed. Free one-hour guided tours are given Saturdays and Sundays at 3. This is almost a mile from town, so figure your travel, visit, and return to London could take about three hours. If you are a lover of 17th- and 18th-century arts, I guarantee you a fulfilling visit.

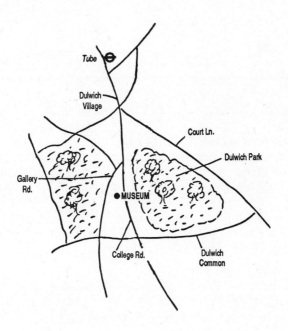

## EPPING FOREST MUSEUM

| | | | |
|---|---|---|---|
| **Open:** | Wed.-Sun. 2-6 | **Type:** | Miscellaneous |
| **Closed:** | Mon., Tues., Major Holidays | **Address:** | Rangers Road, Chingford, E4 7QH |
| **Tube:** | BritRail to Chingford | **Tel:** | 081-529-6681 |
| **Entry:** | £1.00 | | |

Henry VIII loved hunting but was decidedly too heavy to indulge in the sport. He had the Lodge designed, and it was used by himself and his royal party, as a balconied grandstand for viewing staged deer hunts across Chingford Plain. The Tudor design and construction of the Lodge (1543) is still marveled at for its absolute perfection. The museum occupies a portion of the Lodge. Exhibits within show hunting weapons, animal traps, stuffed animals, and drawings of the wonderful wildlife inhabiting the surrounding Epping Forest, originally ten times its present size. The museum and forest are looked after by caring conservationist and environmental groups, giving the museum an affectionate ambiance. At this writing, Epping Forest Lodge is in the midst of its 100-year face lift and will not reopen until 1993.

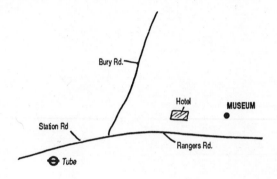

## FAN MUSEUM

| | | | |
|---|---|---|---|
| **Open:** | Tues.-Sat. 11-4:30; Sun. 12-4:30 | **Entry:** | £2.50 |
| | | **Type:** | Miscellaneous |
| **Closed:** | Mondays | **Address:** | 10-12 Crooms Lane, Greenwich, SE10 |
| **Transport:** | River boat to Greenwich Pier | | |
| | | **Tel:** | 081-305-1441 |

For at least 3,000 years the fan has been regarded as a mere fashion accoutrement. Thanks to Mrs. Helene Alexander, whose fan collection forms the nucleus of this museum, all preconceived notions have been discarded. The Fan Museum is located in two beautifully restored elegant Georgian townhouses here in Greenwich, and it is the first and only museum in the world devoted entirely to the fan as a decorative, ceremonial, and functional art form possessing practical and social value. All fans are hand painted, embroidered, or inlaid, and all are well displayed. Workshops and classes are available for fan making; seminars and lectures are held. The museum's back yard has a Parterre garden overlooked by an orangery, which is used for lectures, seminars, social events, and special exhibitions. A tea room and gift shop complete this unusual visit.

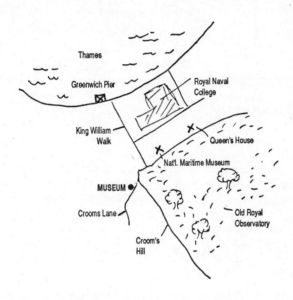

# FLORENCE NIGHTINGALE MUSEUM

| | | | |
|---|---|---|---|
| **Open:** | Tues.-Sun. 10-6 | **Type:** | Individual |
| **Closed:** | Mon., Major Holidays | **Address:** | St. Thomas Hospital, 2 Lambeth Palace Rd., SE1 7EW |
| **Tube:** | Waterloo (Bakerloo, Northern Line) | **Tel:** | 071-620-0374 |
| **Entry:** | £1.00 | | |

Florence Nightingale, the Lady with the Lamp, is one of the world's favorite heroines. This museum was opened in 1989 on the site of St. Thomas' Hospital and is composed of a series of galleries that trace her life from affluent girlhood through young womanhood in the 1850s. Her personal memorabilia and possessions are displayed. A tiny theater shows an audio-visual about her life. In 1854 the Crimean War became the catapulting force for her crusade to improve the nursing profession and health care in hospitals. She established the first school of nursing. During her later years in seclusion, she wrote prolifically, gaining legendary recognition. The museum maintains a Trust for its highly regarded research and value as a resource center. This visit is exciting and interesting, not only for its vivid presentations but for the stirring example set by this remarkable woman who devoted 50 years of her life to a belief.

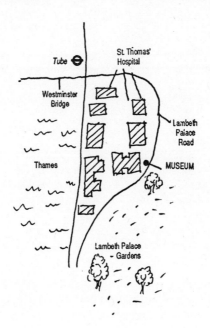

## FREUD MUSEUM

| | | | |
|---|---|---|---|
| **Open:** | Wed.-Sun. 12-5 | **Entry:** | £1.00 |
| **Closed:** | Mon., Tues., | **Type:** | Individual |
| | Major Holidays | **Address:** | 20 Maresfield |
| **Tube:** | Finchley Road | | Gardens, NW3 |
| | (Jubilee, Metro- | | 5SX |
| | politan Line) | **Tel:** | 071-435-2002 |

Sigmund Freud, the illustrious founder of psychoanalysis, fled from Nazi Austria to London in 1938, bringing his extraordinary collection of Egyptian, Greek, Roman, and Oriental antiquities, his furnishings, his library, and his papers. He remained here until his death at 83, one year later. His daughter Anna, a pioneer in childhood psychoanalysis, remained in the house and died here in 1982. Freud's study is intact, from the famous couch draped in a Turkish rug, to his chair behind and his desk, overflowing with countless miniature figures.

Photographs of his family, friends, and colleagues line the walls. The British Psychoanalytic Society holds yearly conferences in London in fitting tribute to Freud. The museum shop offers gifts relating to Freud and his esoteric interests. I recommend a guided tour for further insights into the life of Freud and his complicated and still controversial technique of exploring the human mind.

## GEFFRYE MUSEUM

| | | | |
|---|---|---|---|
| **Open:** | Tues.-Sat. 10-5; Sun. 2-5 | **Entry:** | Free |
| **Closed:** | Mon., Major Holidays | **Type:** | Decorative Arts |
| **Tube:** | Old Street (Northern Line) | **Address:** | Kingsland Road, E2 8EA |
| | | **Tel:** | 071-739-9893 |

This is a museum dedicated mainly to the evolution of the British home and its furnishings, decorative arts, and interior design for middle-class Britain, with exhibits arranged in chronological order from the Tudor era to the 1950s. Its location in Shoreditch is appropriate, since this was London's furniture center during the 18th century. Each of the 14 small period rooms has been recreated to its own specific period and contains appropriate portraits, paintings, and personal touches. Earlier on, the building was an almshouse and hospital, which might account for its design and the almost-chapel behind the center entrance. Those plane trees out front are the originals, planted in 1715. Look over the center doorway to see a statue of Sir Robert Geffrye, the ironmonger who made his fortune in the slavery trade and who subsequently became Lord Mayor of London in 1685. Since it was Mr. Geffrye who founded the almshouse, the museum is named after him.

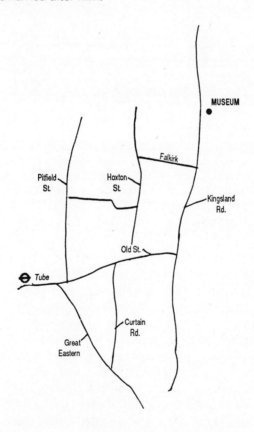

## GEOLOGICAL MUSEUM

| | | | |
|---|---|---|---|
| **Open:** | Mon.-Sat. 10-6; | **Entry:** | £1.00 |
| | Sun. 2:30-6 | **Type:** | Science |
| **Closed:** | Major Holidays | **Address:** | Exhibition Road, |
| **Tube:** | South Kensington | | SW7 2DE |
| | (Piccadilly, | **Tel:** | 071-938-8765 |
| | District Line) | | |

The museum is located in the center of the museum complex, between the Science and Natural History museums. The museum's contents are technical and scholarly, yet there's something here for every level of science student. There are countless exhibitions, thousands of filled glass cases, displays, and galleries featuring minerals, stones, rocks, fossils, and demonstrations of Earth's origin and resources. Don't miss the collection of priceless gemstones, shown both in their natural and their cut states. There's a darkened gallery that tells the enigmatic story of time and space while realistic vibrations duplicate both a volcanic eruption and an earthquake. A visit here is revealing, dramatic, and stimulating to the imagination. Your visit can be combined with a tour of the Science and Natural History museums next door, and why not include the Victoria & Albert across the street?

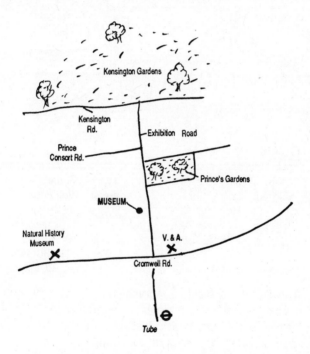

## GUARDS MUSEUM

| | | | |
|---|---|---|---|
| **Open:** | Sat.-Thurs. 10-4 | **Type:** | Military |
| **Closed:** | Fri., Major | **Address:** | Wellington |
| | Holidays | | Barracks, |
| **Tube:** | St. James Park | | Birdcage Walk, |
| | (Circle/District | | SW1E 6HQ |
| | Line) | **Tel:** | 071-930-4466 |
| **Fee:** | £1.00 | | Ext. 3271 |

This is the smallest of London's eight military museums.
Five elite foot guard regiments are represented here—
Grenadiers, Scots, Welsh, Irish, and Coldstream—
distinguished from each other by uniform colors,
insignias, emblems, badges, plume positions, and
particular buttons. The museum, opened in 1988, is
situated in subterranean premises directly beneath the
Wellington Barracks. Three hundred years of history
and tradition chronologically unfold here, with weapons, trophies, paintings, personal belongings, memora-

bilia, and tributes to guardsmen from the 1600s to the Falklands War of 1982. The museum is entirely staffed by retired members of the regiments. The piping in of stirring martial music enhances the museum's patriotic atmosphere. The five represented regiments are the very same guards who participate in the Changing of the Guards ceremony next door at Buckingham Palace—just follow the crowd.

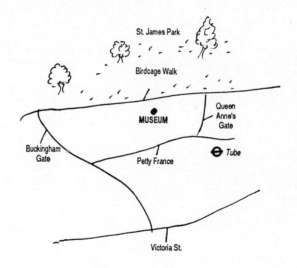

## GUILDHALL CLOCK MUSEUM

| | | | |
|---|---|---|---|
| **Open:** | Mon.-Fri. 9:30-5 | **Type:** | General |
| **Closed:** | Sat., Sun., Major Holidays | **Address:** | Guildhall Library, Aldermanbury, EC 2P |
| **Tube:** | Bank (Central, Northern Line) | **Tel:** | 071-606-3030 Ext. 2868 |
| **Entry:** | Free | | |

The Worshipful Company of Clockmakers was founded in 1630. This one-room museum, a portion of the Guildhall Research Library, contains the Guild's collection of hundreds of hand-crafted watches and clocks. Mechanical clocks appeared in the late 13th century, tiny pocket watches in 1600. They're displayed here, along with 17th- and 18th-century pocket watches, table clocks, and Grandfather clocks. All keep perfect time. One of the more interesting items is a large astronomical table clock, dating from about 1692.

It indicates sunrise, sunset, lunar information, and planetary mathematics and reportedly belonged to Sir Isaac Newton. On occasional Mondays, the clocks are wound, which means the museum closes briefly. This small museum seems peaceful, no doubt because of the soft sound of many clocks ticking.

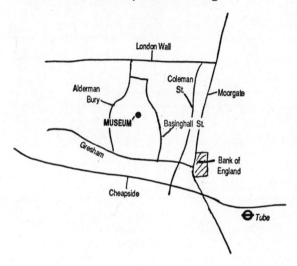

## HAMPTON COURT PALACE

| | | | |
|---|---|---|---|
| **Open:** | Summer: Daily 9:30-6; Winter: Daily 9:30-4 | **Entry:** | £2.50 |
| | | **Type:** | Historic |
| **Closed:** | Major Holidays | **Address:** | East Molesey, Surrey, KT8 9AU |
| **Tube:** | Hampton Court or Railway (Victoria Station) | **Tel:** | 081-977-8441 |

Hampton Court is where English kings and queens from Henry VIII to the 18th century lived and left their indelible marks. It's a vast complex of architecture, personalities, intrigue, lifestyles, buildings, gardens, and eras. Its history could fill a lifetime of study, and the great fire of 1987 unearthed further exciting discoveries from times past. The Palace's design is the epitome of Tudor perfection. Priceless paintings are everywhere, treasures abound. Portraits of the famous and infamous line the walls of the State Apartments.

Hampton is exciting, and it's all true. Two added wonders are the Great Vine, planted in the 1760s and still overflowing with grapes, and the playful Maze. Have lunch in the cafeteria, a short stroll along the River Thames, and you've had a fine day in the country. Did you notice the 24-hour clock in the Clock Court?

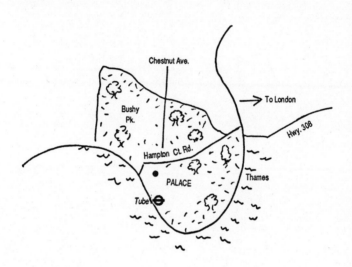

## HOGARTH'S HOUSE MUSEUM

| | | | |
|---|---|---|---|
| **Open:** | Mon., Wed.-Sat. 11-6; Sun 2-6 | **Entry:** | Free |
| **Closed:** | Tues., Holidays; First 2 weeks in Sept.; Dec. | **Type:** | Individual |
| | | **Address:** | Hogarth Lane, Great West Road, W4 2QN |
| **Tube:** | Turnham Green (District Line) | **Tel:** | 081-994-6757 |

William Hogarth was perhaps England's most famous engraver, a genius at the art of cutting a design or image onto a metal plate, then printing that design. He portrayed eighteenth-century England in an illuminating fashion by creating several groups of action within one engraving while disciplining his groups to remain in one central theme. His style remains unmatched. Engraving was not his only claim to fame. He was also a master painter, a relatively little-known fact—that is, until this visit. Some reproductions of his works (two of his most well known are "The Rake's Progress" and "The Harlot's Progress") are here; the originals hang in the Tate, the National Gallery, and Sir John Soane's. This tiny, modest home, squeezed precariously between a main traffic artery and an office building, was his summer residence during the 1750s. That mulberry tree out front, although more than 200 years old, still bears fruit.

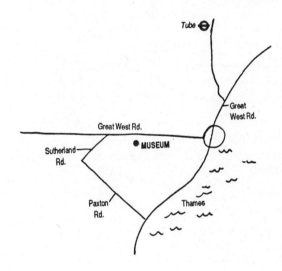

## HORNIMAN MUSEUM AND LIBRARY

| | | | |
|---|---|---|---|
| **Open:** | Tues.-Sat. 10:30-6; Sun. 2-6 | **Entry:** | Free |
| | | **Type:** | General |
| **Closed:** | Major Holidays | **Address:** | 100 London Road, Forest Hill, SE23 3PQ |
| **Transport:** | BritRail, Forest Hill (Waterloo Station) | **Tel:** | 081-699-2339 |

Frederick Horniman, a tea magnate with a special interest in humanities and the arts, was an insatiable collector who traveled around the world gathering treasures. These premises were created for him in 1901, and from the huge mosaic facade to the ponderous walrus out back, including the intimate galleries in between, you've got a highly personalized visit. The museum's three main divisions are Ethnography, Musical Instruments (there are more than 6,000), and Natural History. Galleries are clearly separated with no run-over from one to another. There are also wonderful gardens and a small zoo open dawn to dusk year round. The museum is held dear to the hearts of its devotees—it's one of London's best loved family museums, probably because of its friendly, unpretentious atmosphere. Remember, it's a distance from central London. And don't miss that Apostle Clock on the top floor.

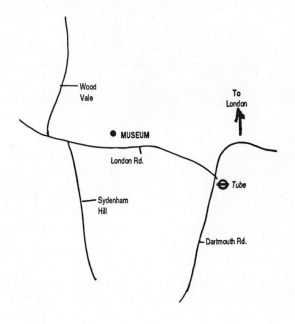

## IMPERIAL WAR MUSEUM

| | | | |
|---|---|---|---|
| **Open:** | Mon.-Sat. 10-6; | **Entry:** | £1.00 |
| | Sun. 2-6 | **Type:** | Military |
| **Closed:** | Major Holidays | **Address:** | Lambeth Road, |
| **Tube:** | Lambeth North | | SE1 6HZ |
| | (Bakerloo Line) | **Tel:** | 071-735-8922 |

This museum deals with all the wars and warfare of the 20th century that involved Britain and her Commonwealth countries. You can't miss the building, with those two 15-inch guns aimed straight at you as you approach. Once inside, there's a sparkling museum, recently renovated. You'll see planes, tanks, anti-aircraft guns, cannon, missiles (V-1 and V-2), a German one-man sub, a Russian MIG, Lawrence of Arabia's rifle, and much more. The 20-minute "London Experience" exhibit, £1 extra, complete with smell, sound,

and terror, is popular—though not for people of
nervous disposition. 1992 will bring another real-life
war thriller called "Trench Experience," no doubt with
equal impact. War paintings and drawings are on the
second floor. A secluded room in one corner of the
main floor shows 12 of J.S. Sargent's Battle Series—
watercolors, pencil drawings, and an immense oil, all
done on site—a little known facet of Sargent's life. The
museum is light, bright, and cleanly done.

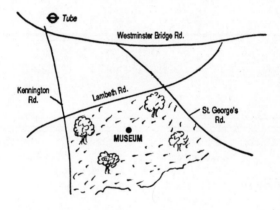

## JEWISH MUSEUM

| | | | |
|---|---|---|---|
| **Open:** | Mon.-Thurs. 10-4; Summer, Fri. 10-12 | **Entry:** | Free (voluntary donation) |
| | | **Type:** | Religious |
| **Closed:** | Fri. afternoon, Sat., Public & Jewish Holidays | **Address:** | Woburn House, Tavistock Square, WC1H OEP |
| **Tube:** | Euston (Northern Line) | **Tel:** | 071-346-2288 |

This one-room museum is crammed full of Jewish art, ritual, religion, history, culture, and understanding. The earliest date represented is about the first century A.D. All of the antiquities in the cases have been obtained from synagogues in and around Europe, where Judaism flourished. Holidays relating to Jewish life are portrayed, with religious articles, cases with carvings, silver, gold, and other religious objects, some set with stones or delicately carved, some created from precious

metals and painted enamel. There are hand-painted
holiday dishes, elaborate Torahs with their covers and
arks, Hanukkah lamps, intricately drawn Ketubahs
(ceremonial marriage contracts), a large selection of
both Hebrew and English books, and religious apparel.
Sit down for a brief film on Jewish ritual and principles.

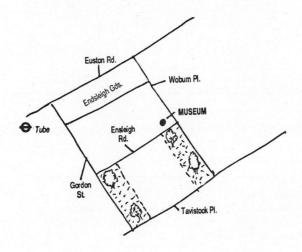

## LEIGHTON HOUSE MUSEUM

| | | | |
|---|---|---|---|
| **Open:** | Mon.-Sat. 11-5 | **Entry:** | Free |
| **Closed:** | Sun., Major | **Type:** | Fine Arts |
| | Holidays | **Address:** | 12 Holland Park |
| **Tube:** | High Street/ | | Road, W14 8LZ |
| | Kensington | **Tel:** | 071-602-3316 |
| | (Circle/District | | |
| | Line) | | |

This was the home and atelier of Lord Leighton,
Victorian artist, President of the Royal Academy of Arts,
and art collector. His collection spans the 30 years
before his death in 1896, an era in art known as High
Victorian. Leighton was a successful painter, and
apparently he traveled extensively to the Mediterra-
nean, the Near East, and Africa because the museum is
filled with decorative and exotic arts, mosaic floors and
walls, Moorish, Moslem, and Arabic arts and furnishings in heavy silks, damasks, and intricate carpets. The

museum contains many of Leighton's exotic paintings and those of his contemporaries. His studio, overflowing with Victorian accoutrements, has been faithfully preserved. Leighton House has recently been renovated, all the better for the lushness herein. The exotic theme continues upstairs, where private concerts are held. The gardens behind the house have several sculptures, some by Lord Leighton, others by his colleagues. Here is one of London's more interesting "undiscovered" museums.

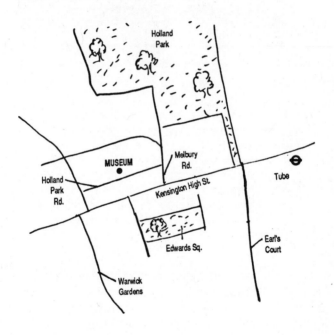

## LONDON PLANETARIUM AND LASERIUM

| | | | |
|---|---|---|---|
| **Open:** | Daily 10-5; Weekends 9:30-5:30 | **Entry:** | £3.50—Share ticket with Madame Tussaud's |
| **Closed:** | Christmas | | |
| **Tube:** | Baker Street (Jubilee, Metropolitan Line) | **Type:** | Miscellaneous |
| | | **Address:** | Marylebone Road, NW1 5LR |
| | | **Tel:** | 071-486-1121 |

0207 9356861

I can't imagine who engineered the marriage between Madame Tussaud and the Planetarium. They not only share close quarters but one ticket gets you into both places. At any rate, you can't miss the Laserium's copper-green dome looming over the area. In addition to innumerable presentations about the wonders of the universe, the ground floor, invariably filled with high-energy visitors, has an Astronomers Gallery, demonstrating mind-boggling discoveries. In the evenings the

Planetarium theater becomes the Laserium, turning into a virtual paradise of fantasy in laser light accompanied by music, from classical to rock/pop, with three different shows to choose among. Ride the galaxy for your eclectic journey through time and space. Sundays and holidays are popular, so get in line. The Gift Shop has thousands of small gifts.

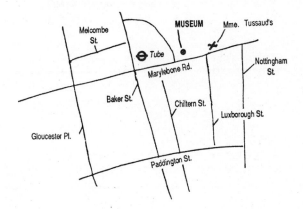

## LONDON TOY & MODEL MUSEUM

| | | | |
|---|---|---|---|
| **Open:** | Tues.-Sat. 10-5:30; Sun. 11-5:30 | **Entry:** | £1.00 |
| | | **Type:** | Children's |
| **Closed:** | Mon., Major Holidays | **Address:** | 21 Craven Hill, W2 3EN |
| **Tube:** | Lancaster Gate (Central Line) | **Tel:** | 071-262-7905 |

London is one of the few cities in the world with museums dedicated to and solely for children. This is one of them. Two elegant Victorian buildings house the collection built on memories, spanning two centuries and holding thousands of toys and models, including trains, boats, planes, model cars and fire engines, soldiers, dolls and dollhouses, puppets, a toy fort, bears and other toy animals—all behind glass. There are two floors of galleries filled with cases following particular themes of juvenalia. Outside in the back yard there's a ride-on steam train, an Edwardian merry-go-round, a play bus, a boat pond, and a picnic area. Both adults' and kids' favorite choices are the Model Train and the Teddy Bear rooms. The Clockwork Cafe upstairs is a sweet little place for your snack. The museum offers an outstanding variety of year-round, highly popular shows and events especially for kids.

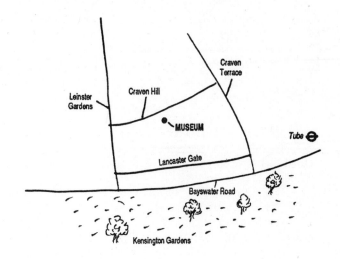

## LONDON TRANSPORT MUSEUM

| | | | |
|---|---|---|---|
| **Open:** | Daily 10-6 | **Entry:** | £1.00 |
| **Closed:** | Christmas, | **Type:** | General |
| | Boxing Day (first | **Address:** | The Piazza, |
| | weekday after | | Covent Garden, |
| | Christmas) | | WC2E 7BB |
| **Tube:** | Covent Garden | **Tel:** | 071-379-6344 |
| | (Piccadilly Line) | | |

This is one of London's popular family museums and literally great fun for kids of all ages, with buses, trolley-buses, trams, trains, train models, coaches and carriages, and all sorts of vehicles—some to climb on, some to participate in, and some for touch. The Victorian building was formerly London's flower market, with high ceilings and plenty of window light. London's transport system has always been well thought of, and the museum explains why, with exhibits showing the development of the system in drawings, illustrations and posters, photos and memorabilia. Every vehicle is sparklingly polished. Weekends are given over to special films and activities. The energy level is high at all times, and there's plenty of dashing about. The immediate area, Covent Garden, lends an atmosphere of excitement to the museum. Why not allow your family some extra time for strolling, shopping, or eating in the neighborhood?

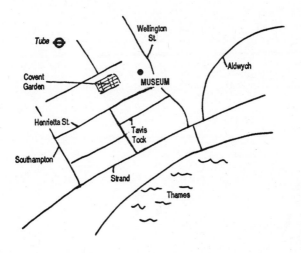

## LONDON ZOO

| | | | |
|---|---|---|---|
| **Open:** | Summer: Daily 9-Dark; Winter: Daily 10-Dark | **Entry:** | £3.50 |
| | | **Type:** | Children's |
| | | **Address:** | Regents Park, NW1 |
| **Closed:** | Christmas | | |
| **Tube:** | Regent's Park (Bakerloo Line) | **Tel:** | 071-722-3333 |

This may not be the world's largest zoo but it's one of the oldest and one of the best. It's up in the northeastern corner of Regent's Park. First of all, it's refreshing to be able to escape from London's hectic pace and turn to this peaceful environment where animals are oblivious to hordes of visitors. Six thousand animals live here on 35 acres, and if you like, you can adopt one of them. For an extra donation of £13 a year, adopt a jellyfish. For £1250 you can adopt a giraffe. Here, also, is where those two giant pandas from China now live. The real Keeper of the Zoo is the Royal Zoological Society, and this site is their private garden and research institute. Traditional animal cages have given way to natural-habitat settings, so animals do roam about happily. Regent's Park beckons for a stroll, perhaps to the Boating Lake—then to Queen Mary's Gardens for a snack—and the end of a perfect day out-of-doors.

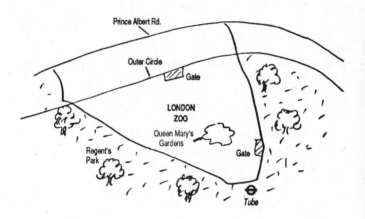

## MADAME TUSSAUD'S WAXWORKS

| | | | |
|---|---|---|---|
| **Open:** | Daily 10-5:30; Weekends 9:30-5:30 | **Entry:** | £3.50—Share Ticket with Planetarium |
| **Closed:** | Major Holidays | **Type:** | Miscellaneous |
| **Tube:** | Baker Street (Jubilee, Metropolitan Line) | **Address:** | Marylebone Road, NW1 5LR |
| | | **Tel:** | 071-935-6861 |

Of all the waxwork museums in the world, Madame Tussaud's in London leads the pack. It's surely the best known and hardly "undiscovered." There really was a Madame Tussaud. Her illustrious career began in Versailles, then moved to Paris into the court of Louis XVI, where business flourished as long as the guillotine did. The Revolution hastened her departure to London around 1800, and her technique of people-preservation accompanied her. She even reproduced herself, placing her image in the Famous Rulers Room. There's an upstairs workshop where new figures are made. Start at the top floor and work your way down. You can pick your favorite scenario, although the gruesome Chamber of Horrors rates as the general public's all-time favorite. Sound effects are imaginative, *haut drame* prevails; there's rumor of a smellorama machine in the woodwork of the waxworks. This is the biggest hit in town, so be prepared for chaos and a high noise level.

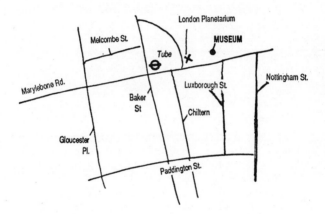

## MUSEUM OF ARTILLERY IN THE ROTUNDA

| | | | |
|---|---|---|---|
| **Open:** | Daily 12-5; Sat., Sun. 1-5 | **Type:** | Military |
| **Closed:** | Major Holidays | **Address:** | Repository Road, Woolwich, SE18 4DN |
| **Tube:** | Woolwich Arsenal Station | **Tel:** | 081-854-2242 Ext. 3127 |
| **Entry:** | Free | | |

Have you ever wondered who came up with the notion
of artillery, small weapons and cannon, how the
technology developed, and so on? The answers are
here. The history of weaponry is traced in this Rotunda,
designed in 1820 by John Nash. It's a striking circular
tent covered with a lead roof and placed amidst
Woolwich's Artillery Barracks. Simple guns came into
use around the 14th century and have grown with
passing wars and years into today's sophisticated
weapons. It is in fact wars that dictate the need for

changes in weaponry. Included in the museum are the evolution of small arms, machine guns, anti-aircraft guns, rockets, small arms, cannon, and diverse varieties of weaponry. Apparently a cannon's true value is determined by its performance in terms of inflicted casualties, per graphic photos and drawings. This is a great place for the military enthusiast.

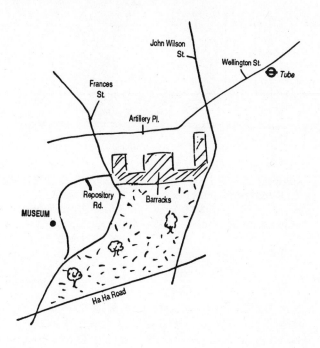

## MUSEUM OF GARDEN HISTORY

| | | | |
|---|---|---|---|
| **Open:** | Mon.-Fri. 11-3; Sun. 10:30-5 | **Entry:** | Free |
| | | **Type:** | Miscellaneous |
| **Closed:** | Sat.; Dec. through Mar. | **Address:** | St. Mary-at-Lambeth, |
| **Tube:** | Westminster (Circle/District Line) | | Lambeth Palace Road, SE1 7JU |
| | | **Tel:** | 071-261-1891 |

John Tradescant and his son John were 17th-century gardeners to Charles I and several notable patrons of the art of horticulture. They traveled to Europe, North Africa, Russia, and the United States, buying specimens of trees, plants, and shrubs, and introduced plantings never before seen in England. The museum, which is one large room housed in a former parish church, exudes a simple innocent joy. Techniques of gardening and aspects of gardening history are shown. Its exhibits are a visual pleasure, the gift shop has its own special personality, and the tea room, in a corner of the museum, offers home-made snacks. A stroll out the back door leads into the gardens, where a corner set aside in memory of John and his son incorporates some of the original strains of plantings from three centuries ago. Do you wonder why Captain Bligh is buried in these gardens alongside the Tradescant family?

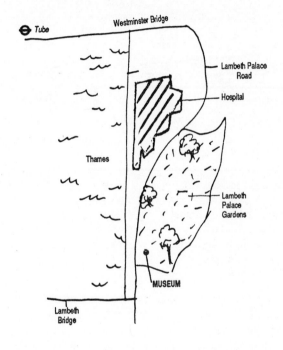

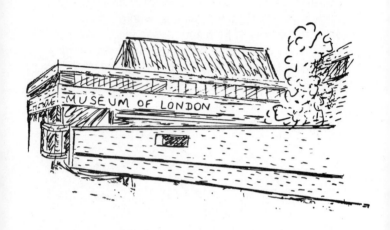

## MUSEUM OF LONDON

| | | | |
|---|---|---|---|
| **Open:** | Tues.-Sat. 10-6; Sun. 2-6 | **Entry:** | Free |
| **Closed:** | Monday, Major Holidays | **Type:** | Historic |
| | | **Address:** | London Wall, EC2Y 5HN |
| **Tube:** | Barbican (Circle, Metropolitan Line) | **Tel:** | 071-600-3699 |

This museum presents a complete sociological record of London's fine arts, performing arts, cultural heritage, and craftsmanship. There's something here for everyone. All departments are collected from archaeological excavations and are arranged chronologically, beginning with Prehistoric and Roman London, through Medieval London, Tudor/Stuart London, up to Modern London. The Tudor/Stuart galleries portray life in London during the 16th and 17th centuries. One of the public's favorites is the re-creation of London's Great

Fire of 1666 by means of an audio-visual program. The Costume segment, the paintings, prints, and drawings only add to the museum's luster. As a matter of fact, this is one of London's finer museums, and the best thing about this museum is what it's not—overbearing and tiresome. Bravo for a job well done! And don't let the modern exterior design fool you. This is a classic historical museum. Do not miss the tiny Music Room, lower level.

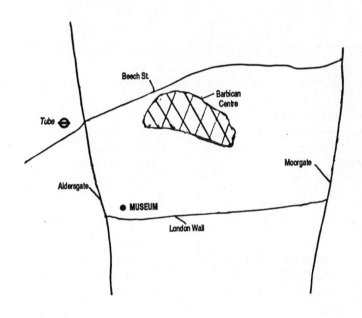

## MUSEUM OF MANKIND

| | | | |
|---|---|---|---|
| **Open:** | Mon.-Sat. 10-5;<br>Sun. 2:30-6 | **Entry:**<br>**Type:** | Free<br>Science |
| **Closed:** | Major Holidays | **Address:** | 6 Burlington |
| **Tube:** | Piccadilly Circus<br>(Piccadilly,<br>Bakerloo Line) | | Gardens, W1X<br>2EX |
| | | **Tel:** | 071-437-2224 |

Welcome. Your entrance is greeted by the towering figure of an Easter Island resident. This museum is the Ethnographic Department of the British Museum, even though the two are separated by a mile or so. It illustrates a variety of non-Western tribal societies and cultures, ancient and recent, including Aztec, Mayan, African, Asian, Oceanian, and Middle Eastern. Briefly, the museum is recognized as a major center for cultural anthropology. Changing exhibits are selected from the British Museum's permanent collection. Costume and

very special visual and sound effects. It's not only educational but it's entertaining. The museum is constantly winning prestigious awards, and it's easy to see why. It's a House of Illusion. Cameras and filming equipment, nostalgic photos of early movie mogul days, plus a movie theater, and much more. Seeing is believing, so fasten your seat belt. This is a bumpy ride, and you get your money's worth all the way.

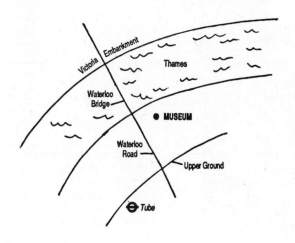

## MUSICAL MUSEUM

| | | | |
|---|---|---|---|
| **Open:** | Sat. & Sun. 2-5 | **Address:** | 368 High Street, |
| **Tube:** | Gunnersbury | | Brentford, |
| | (District Line) | | Middlesex, TW8 |
| **Entry:** | £1.00 | | OBD |
| **Type:** | Miscellaneous | **Tel:** | 081-560-8108 |

This is an odd place for a museum to be—in a former 19th-century church, but it's lovely and the acoustics are excellent. It's a collection of automated musical instruments from the 19th and 20th centuries, not unlike the Musee Mecanique in Paris. Its star attraction is the Welte Philharmonic Reproducing Pipe Organ, with no less than 471 pipes in 10 ranks, and it plays rolls performed by some of the finest organ musicians of a bygone era. Take an hour and a half for a fully explained tour conducted by Mr. Holland, the founder of the museum, complete with demonstrations. You'll see and hear barrel organs, player pianos, phonographs, music boxes, and orchestrions. Their stories are sensitively narrated, with detailed historical background. What a collection of musicology! If you stop by the gift shop, you can buy some charming and unique gifts—how about a piano roll to start?

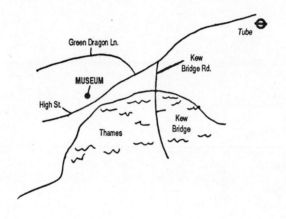

## NATIONAL ARMY MUSEUM

| | | | |
|---|---|---|---|
| **Open:** | Mon.-Sat. 10-5:30; Sun. 2-5:30 | **Entry:** | Free |
| | | **Type:** | Military |
| **Closed:** | Major Holidays | **Address:** | Royal Hospital Road, Chelsea, SW3 4HT |
| **Tube:** | Sloane Square (Circle/District Line) | | |
| | | **Tel:** | 071-730-0717 |

Just look for Wren's Royal Hospital beside the River—this museum is next door. It's not only a military museum but also a visual documentation of the British Army from the mid-1400s under Henry VII through worldwide campaigns, including those of the Indian Army and other colonial forces, the Falklands conflict of 1982, and all battles in between. England's pride in her military is evident here. The museum tells the human side of soldiering with sensitivity, admiration, and respect. There are several galleries of weapons and uniforms and a vast collection of medals, trophies, badges, and relics. Special exhibitions are held several times a year, which recreate not only the atmosphere of war but capture the compelling spirit of the British soldier. The museum is the major national archive for all military manuscripts, drawings, prints, photos, and paintings. Like all of London's military museums, it's sharp and well done.

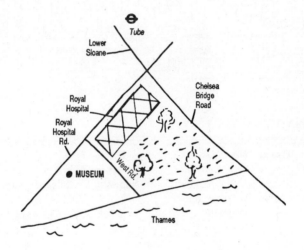

## NATIONAL GALLERY

| | | | |
|---|---|---|---|
| **Open:** | Mon.-Sat. 10-6; Sun. 2-6 | **Entry:** | Free |
| **Closed:** | Major Holidays | **Type:** | Fine Arts |
| **Tube:** | Leicester Square (Piccadilly, Northern Line) | **Address:** | Trafalgar Square, WC2N 5BN |
| | | **Tel:** | 071-839-3321 |

The National Gallery is one of the most important picture galleries in the world, housing more than 2,000 fabulous paintings dating from the 13th to the 20th century—all masterpieces, and complemented by furnishings and decorative arts. This is unquestionably an example of how a fine art gallery can flourish. Nothing has been overlooked in content and presentation, so leave yourself enough time for full immersion— it will take your breath away. Impressionists are downstairs. Their Artist in Residence program allows an artist to work in one of the Gallery's studios for six months, during which time one day a week is devoted to conversations with visitors. The remainder of time is spent painting. Coming in 1991 are not only an auditorium and additional galleries but the significant Sainsbury Wing, containing Italian Renaissance works prior to the 16th century, a collection till now not seen outside of Florence. This promises to bring the National Gallery to a spectacular level of grandeur. Now here's the way to spend a day.

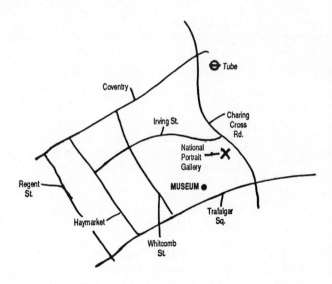

## NATIONAL MARITIME MUSEUM

| | | | |
|---|---|---|---|
| **Open:** | Mon.-Sat. 10-6; | **Entry:** | £1.00 |
| | Sun. 2-8; Winter: | **Type:** | Military |
| | Mon.-Sat. 10-5; | **Address:** | Romney Road, |
| | Sun. 2-5 | | Greenwich Park, |
| **Closed:** | Major Holidays | | SE10 9NF |
| **Transport:** | River Boat to | **Tel:** | 071-858-4422 |
| | Greenwich Pier | | |

That England was Queen of the Seas is indisputably evident here, in this museum's splendid coverage of her sea power, naval warfare, the shipping industry, their roles in British history, and two galleries devoted to that great naval hero, Lord Nelson (1758–1805). This is the largest maritime museum in the world. Its spacious galleries are filled with ship models, maps, navigational equipment, and naval weapons. There are exhibits on shipbuilding techniques, maritime archaeology, commercial fishing and whaling, yachting, and

Arctic exploration. Downstairs are real ships—plus paintings, prints, drawings, photographs, and relics. A fun part of your visit should be a walk through the paddle tugboat "Reliant" (1907) exhibited in the Neptune Hall. This museum has recently been refurbished, along with the Queen's House, just next door. The Old Royal Observatory is across the meadow and a short climb to the top of the hill.

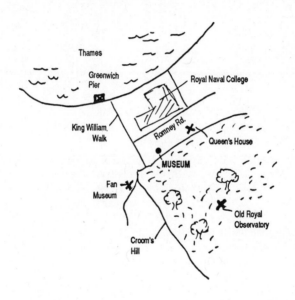

## NATIONAL PORTRAIT GALLERY

| | | | |
|---|---|---|---|
| **Open:** | Mon.-Fri. 10-5; Sat. 10-6; Sun. 2-6; Winter: Mon.-Sat. 10-5; Sun. 2-5 | **Entry:** | Free |
| | | **Type:** | Fine Arts |
| | | **Address:** | St. Martin's Place, WC2H OHE |
| **Closed:** | Major Holidays | | |
| **Tube:** | Leicester Square (Bakerloo, Northern Line) | **Tel:** | 071-930-1552 |

The Gallery gives you precisely what it says it will: portraits and portraits only—more than 10,000 of them—all British. Not only are there paintings but also photographs, sculptured heads, and drawings. Begin your visit on the top floor and work chronologically down. At every turn you will be surrounded by history in images. And what better way to discover Britain's history than through the people who lived it? Every imaginable style of portraiture is here, and the combination is positively exciting. Temporary exhibitions are guaranteed to be top class. Every year in June the Gallery holds an exciting event aimed at gifted young portraiture artists. It's the prestigious Portrait Award, open only to British and Commonwealth citizens, and it involves liberal cash prizes. The Gallery Shop, one of London's better gift shops, offers an impressive number and variety of books, prints, postal cards, posters, and slides.

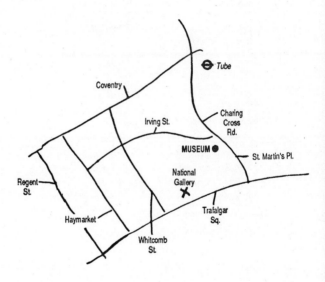

## NATIONAL POSTAL MUSEUM

| | | | |
|---|---|---|---|
| **Open:** | Mon.-Thur. 10-4:30; Fri. 10-4 | **Entry:** | Free |
| | | **Type:** | General |
| **Closed:** | Sat., Sun., Major Holidays | **Address:** | King Edward Street, EC1A 1LP |
| **Tube:** | St. Paul's (Central Line) | **Tel:** | 071-239-5420 |

This is a pure paradise for philatelists. Enter through the main entrance of the Chief Post Office building, then climb three flights of steps to the main gallery. Here is the history of mail service in England, begun in 1840. You'll also find a stamp collection reputed to be the largest and most important in the world, with stamps from rare private collections. You'll discover how stamps are designed and produced. Ever changing temporary exhibitions are obtained from the official postal archives. Library and research facilities are offered. The museum's private Berne collection is huge, historical, and highly regarded. Apparently, there's a large community of stamp collectors and connoisseurs in London, for this museum is very well attended by that group.

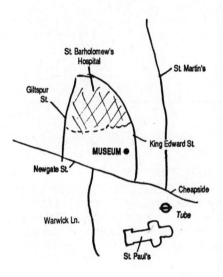

## NATURAL HISTORY MUSEUM

| | | | |
|---|---|---|---|
| **Open:** | Mon.-Sat. 10-6;<br>Sun. 1-6 | **Entry:**<br>**Type:** | £1.00<br>Science |
| **Closed:** | Major Holidays | **Address:** | Cromwell Road, |
| **Tube:** | South Kensington<br>(Piccadilly,<br>District Line) | **Tel:** | SW7 5BD<br>071-725-7866 |

This is a branch of the British Museum and one of
London's most flamboyant museum buildings, with its
spires and towers and facings of pastel tiles. There's
something awesome in this temple of natural history. Its
exhibits include the continents before humans arose,
human evolution and history of man, treasures within
the earth, creatures who inhabit the earth above
ground, below ground, and beneath the sea, and bird
life. The number of species is enormous, but you can
always seek out the Charles Darwin exhibition for an

understandable simplification. Dinosaur buffs are ecstatic. In the Story of the Earth exhibit, the story of our planet from its formation billions of years ago is told. A current presentation is called Britain's Offshore Oil & Gas, designed in the form of a double-decked oil platform. This museum was the dream and realization of Prince Albert, consort of Queen Victoria. Would you believe there are more than 15 million species within these walls? The visitor is not obliged to find or count them all.

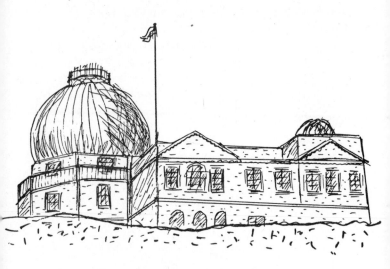

## OLD ROYAL OBSERVATORY (Greenwich)

| | | | |
|---|---|---|---|
| **Open:** | Mon.-Sat. 10-6; Sun. 2-6 | **Type:** | Science |
| **Closed:** | Major Holidays | **Address:** | Greenwich Park, Greenwich, SE10 9NF |
| **Transport:** | River Boat to Greenwich Pier | **Tel:** | 071-858-4422 |
| **Entry:** | £1.00 | | |

You will see the imposing Observatory dome at the top of the hill as you approach from the river boat. Zero meridian, the point from which time and the two hemispheres begin, is indicated by a brass strip running along the courtyard ground. World clocks, maps, charts, transportation systems, and military communities operate on Greenwich Mean Time's 24-hour principle. Frampton House galleries, next door, are filled with clocks, watches, sextants, cosmic clockworks, sundials, astronomical instruments, astrolabes, and various other simple and complex attempts to define time. What an assortment, and all fashioned with absolute precision! The original Greenwich Telescope sits here, too. As you leave, notice the immense 24-hour clock, not unlike the one at Hampton Court Palace. The nearby planetarium has programs on the celestial heavens.

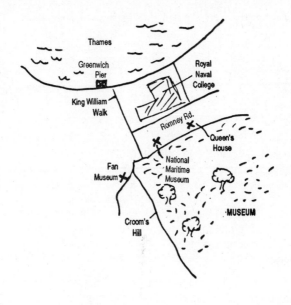

## PETRIE MUSEUM OF EGYPTOLOGY

| | | | |
|---|---|---|---|
| **Open:** | Mon.-Fri. 10-12; 1-5 | **Entry:** | Free |
| | | **Type:** | Science |
| **Closed:** | Major Holidays, one month during summer | **Address:** | University College, Gower St., WC1E 6BT |
| **Tube:** | Euston (Northern Line) | **Tel:** | 071-387-7050 Ext. 2884 |

The museum, a division of the Department of
Egyptology of London's University College, consists of
two rooms filled with archaeological treasures in
display cases. It takes a bit of doing to find the museum. Once out of the Underground, walk all the way
around and back into the center of the University. The
collection is derived from archaeologists William Petrie
and Amelia Edwards, who unearthed this wealth of
cultural artifacts and antiquities now used for research
and teaching purposes within the University. The

collection illustrates the development of Egyptian culture from the Paleolithic to Roman times. One of the most extraordinary exhibits is the monumental Koptos lions and linen funereal robes belonging to Tarkhan and Deshasheh, circa 3000 B.C.! This small museum is not only for the scholarly student of Egyptology but also for the curious who wonder about the enigmatic and esoteric culture of ancient Egypt.

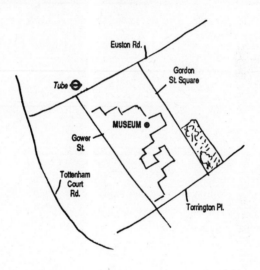

## POLLOCK'S TOY MUSEUM

| | | | |
|---|---|---|---|
| **Open:** | Mon.-Sat. 10-5 | **Entry:** | £1.00 |
| **Closed:** | Sun., Bank | **Type:** | Children's |
| | Holidays | **Address:** | 1 Scala Street, |
| **Tube:** | Goodge Street | | W1P 1LJ |
| | (Northern Line) | **Tel:** | 071-636-3452 |

You can't easily walk past this irresistible red brick building, wrapped around the corner with its large windows crammed full of toys. Benjamin Pollock, who manufactured toy theaters, founded this tiny three-story museum at the turn of the 20th century. It has a dollhouse-like quality, with small rooms connected by narrow winding staircases, more intriguing for small children than the spacious halls of conventional museums. Pollock's has toys from the world over and from all times. Puppets, games, dolls and dollhouses, folk toys, rocking horses, and stuffed animals, all in glass cases and untouchable, fill the museum—a visual feast. Each floor is crammed full of toy wonders, even toy theaters and a toy workshop. The Toyshop sells replicas of almost everything in the museum. This is one of London's special museums for kids.

## PUBLIC RECORD OFFICE MUSEUM

| | | | |
|---|---|---|---|
| **Open:** | Mon.-Fri. 1-4 | **Type:** | Miscellaneous |
| **Closed:** | Sat., Sun., Major Holidays | **Address:** | Chancery Lane, WC2A 1LR |
| **Tube:** | Chancery Lane (Central Line) | **Tel:** | 071-405-0741 Ext. 229 |
| **Entry:** | Free | | |

PRO, as the museum is known, holds the preserved records of Britain's government and Courts of Law from the very beginning of record keeping. Documents range from the Domesday Book, England's land and resource survey commanded by William the Conqueror in 1085, to modern papers, Chancery writings, taxes, and accounts from the 12th century, international treaties, royal court papers, recorded colonial history, official war records, political speeches, trade and transport laws, public health and civil rights documents, genealogical records, all sorts of records from courts of law, and much more. The Magna Carta is here; so is Shakespeare's will, Mrs. Thatcher's debates, and Lord Nelson's "Victory" log, recording the battle of Trafalgar, where he lost his life. All this is in one rather drab room. Do not attempt to remember all you see and read; just enjoy the historical riches around you.

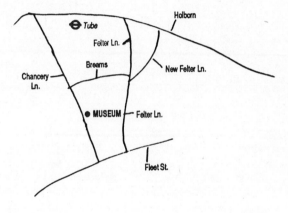

## QUEEN'S GALLERY (Buckingham Palace)

| | | | |
|---|---|---|---|
| **Open:** | Tues.-Sat. 11-5; Sun. 2-5 | **Entry:** | £1.00 |
| **Closed:** | Monday, Christmas, Good Friday | **Type:** | General |
| | | **Address:** | Buckingham Palace, SW1A 1AA |
| **Tube:** | Victoria (Victoria, Circle Line) | **Tel:** | 071-930-4832 |

This is one of London's elegant small museums, tucked into a corner of Buckingham Palace. As in all Royal Family matters, it draws wide interest. It was formerly the private Royal Chapel and after being destroyed during an air raid in WWII, was converted into this gallery for displaying personal Royal Collections. Furniture, porcelains, gold-encrusted jewelry, ceramics, tapestries, paintings, and other luxurious works of art gathered by past royalty are proudly revealed. Each exhibition stays about one year. Since most of these treasures are rarely seen outside Buckingham Palace, this is probably the closest you'll get to glimpsing the personal taste of England's royalty. Be sure to spend time in the museum shop, which, aside from the Botanic Gardens, has one of the city's better assortments of garden and gardening books, cards, and gifts. The Royal Mews is just outside and next door.

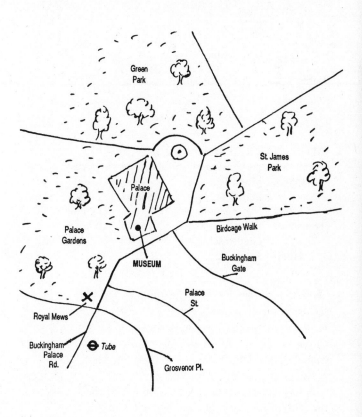

## QUEEN'S HOUSE (Greenwich)

| | | | |
|---|---|---|---|
| **Open:** | Mon.-Sat. 10-6; Sun. 2-6 | **Type:** | General |
| **Closed:** | Major Holidays | **Address:** | Romney Road, Greenwich, SE10 9NF |
| **Transport:** | River Boat to Greenwich Pier | **Tel:** | 071-858-4422 |
| **Entry:** | £1.50 | | |

This stately mansion was designed in 1614 by Inigo Jones, one of London's gifted 17th-century architects. It was commissioned by Charles I as a gift for his consort, Queen Anne of Denmark. After Anne died, Charles married Henrietta Maria, who then became Queen Mistress of the villa. It's a magnificent Palladian palace that has recently been beautifully refurbished. There are three floors to this villa, so look into all those elegant rooms in the West Wing, the East Wing, and of course upstairs. The lower level has galleries with gold

and silver treasures and memorabilia of those past royal
residents. A brief film narrates the history of these royal
tenants. Stop in at the gift shop on the lower floor,
which, aside from traditional gift cards, wrapping
paper, and books, sells preserves, table delicacies, and
wines—all home made in the nearby countryside. And
don't miss the Tulip Staircase.

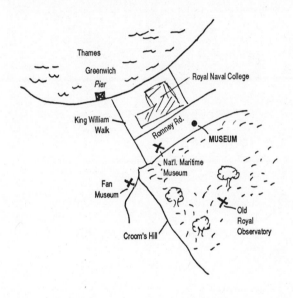

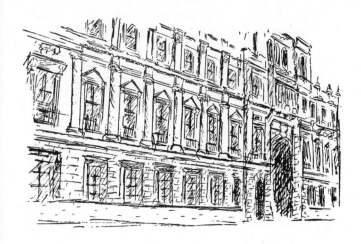

## ROYAL ACADEMY OF ARTS

| | | | |
|---|---|---|---|
| **Open:** | During Exhibitions | **Type:** | Fine Arts |
| **Tube:** | Piccadilly Circus (Piccadilly, Northern Line) | **Address:** | Burlington House, Piccadilly, SW1V ODS |
| **Entry:** | £2.50 | **Tel:** | 071-439-7438 |

The prestigious Academy, founded in 1768, serves three purposes: it's a school of art, a gallery for the display of art and art works, and an arena for promoting young, upcoming artists. The museum is but a small portion of the Academy, whose membership is strictly limited to painters, engravers, sculptors, and architects. An elected President conducts the institution's business. The first floor of the Academy holds a superb Masters permanent collection. The Academy promotes events year round, with special emphasis on their

Summer Exhibition, held June through August, a competition among the *crème de la crème* of aspirants in sculpture, painting, architecture, and engraving. It is only during these competitions that the Academy is open to the public. Their museum shop sells books and gifts, cards, posters, art supplies, and—surprise—spirits bearing the Royal Academy label. Do visit.

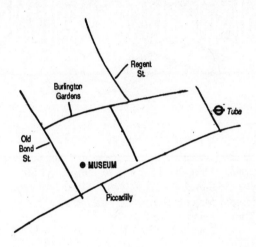

## ROYAL AIR FORCE MUSEUM

| | | | |
|---|---|---|---|
| **Open:** | Mon.-Sat. 10-6; Sun. 2-6 | **Entry:** | £1.50 |
| | | **Type:** | Military |
| **Closed:** | Major Holidays | **Address:** | Hendon, NW9 |
| **Tube:** | Hendon (North-ern Line) | | 5LL |
| | | **Tel:** | 081-205-2266 |

Two hangars at Old Hendon Airfield form the background of this spirited testimonial to the story of
military flight and the history and development of the
RAF, portrayed with its weapons, its way of life, its men
and machines. More than three dozen historic aircraft
plus WWII fighter planes from Britain, Germany, and
Italy sit proudly on display in the Aircraft Hall. Galleries commemorate the Battle of Britain and its stunning
air battles with the Luftwaffe during the summer of
1940. Dramatic sound effects of low-flying aircraft and

air raid sirens add realism to the atmosphere. The upstairs gallery has portraits and sculptures of flying heroes and a cinema for aerial films. England's grand hero, Winston Churchill, is ever present. Like all of London's military museums, this is exhilarating. Future plans are being made to include a Bomber Command Museum. The Battle of Britain Museum is in the same complex. Why not visit it as well? There's no extra charge.

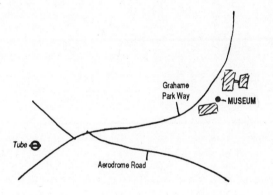

## ROYAL BOTANIC GARDENS (Kew Gardens)

| | | | |
|---|---|---|---|
| **Open:** | Daily: Summer 10-8; Winter: 10 4 | **Tube:** | Kew Gardens (District Line) |
| | | **Entry:** | £1.00 |
| **Closed:** | Christmas, New Years, Boxing Day | **Type:** | Miscellaneous |
| | | **Address:** | Richmond, Surrey, TW9 3AB |
| | | **Tel:** | 081-940-1171 |

This vast park, also known as Kew Gardens, was started 250 years ago. There are five separate entrances, fourteen assorted gardens, a lake, two ponds, six glasshouse/greenhouses (tripods and easels are permitted inside), twenty varieties of plant galleries and hothouses, three restaurants, and the Orangery Gift Shop, all spread over nearly 300 acres. The most recent addition is the Princess of Wales Conservatory, a complex plant house with an immense tropical plant collection. Kew Palace, the original royal residence,

1631, is open April through September. The Queen's Cottage (1770) is open summer weekends and holidays. Don't miss the Pagoda, that intricate, towering garden ornament (1761). Kew's terrain, with its landscaped trees, shrubs, and flowers, is beautifully done. Kew is also a technical scientific research center. All this plus glorious bird life, and only 15 minutes from downtown. The Orangery Gift Shop is one of the best in all of London and its environs.

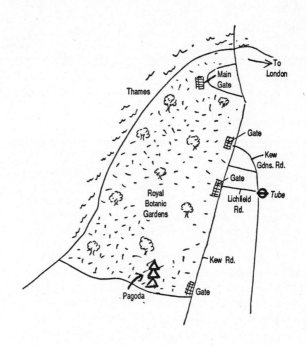

## ROYAL MEWS (Buckingham Palace)

| | | | |
|---|---|---|---|
| **Open:** | Wed., Thurs. 2-4 | **Entry:** | £1.00 |
| **Closed:** | Ascot Week, | **Type:** | Miscellaneous |
| | State Visits, | **Address:** | Buckingham |
| | Major Holidays | | Palace, SW1W |
| **Tube:** | Victoria (Victoria, | | OQH |
| | Circle Line) | **Tel:** | 071-930-4832 |

Traditional and ceremonial pageantry associated with
England's royal mystique prevails here at the stables
and coach house of Buckingham Palace. Enter the
quadrangle, where elegant and elaborate state and
ceremonial coaches, horse-drawn vehicles, and horses
are on display in full regalia. Each coach serves its own
purpose. That is, the coach used for greeting a foreign
Head of State is never used for Royal Weddings, a
Coronation, or an opening of Parliament. Then move
on to the Queen's horses, tack shop, and the saddlery

gallery. The Old Coach House has photographs and medals lining the walls. In August, September, and early October only a small number of horses are here. That's because they are out to pasture. Notice the limited hours and days of opening for this museum. The Card Shop, although tiny, is almost always crowded, no doubt due to its collection—the subject is English royalty. Also, the Mews is closed during Ascot Week in June.

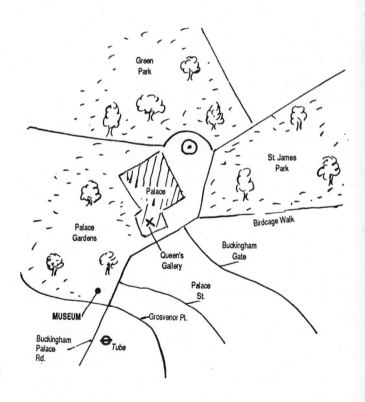

## ST. PAUL'S CATHEDRAL

| | | | |
|---|---|---|---|
| **Open:** | Galleries & Crypt Mon.-Fri. 10-5; Sat., Sun. 11-5 | **Entry:** | Free |
| | | **Type:** | Religious |
| **Tube:** | St. Paul's (Central Line) | **Address:** | St. Paul's Churchyard |

Although St. Paul's is not a museum, I have included it in this book because the church is one of London's architectural masterpieces, redesigned by Sir Christopher Wren after the 1666 fire. St. Paul's was, as a matter of fact, Wren's favorite design. He rests in the Crypt. Aside from being the resting place for some of England's most illustrious military heroes (Britain's Unknown Soldier, the Duke of Wellington, and Lord Nelson lie buried under the massive dome), tribute is paid to British forces the world over. St. Paul's also has its Artists' Corner, in which Turner, Lawrence, and Reynolds are buried. During WWII, St. Paul's and its dome became London's heroic symbol of survival. If you're lucky enough to hear the boys' choir during services, your visit will be significantly enriched. There's a low-priced, hour-and-a-half tour, which guides you into some of the hidden corners and offers otherwise unknown historic stories connected with St. Paul's.

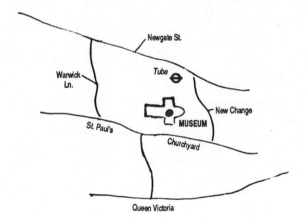

## SCIENCE MUSEUM

| Open: | Mon.-Sat. 10-6; | Entry: | £1.00 |
|---|---|---|---|
| | Sun. 11-6 | Type: | Science |
| Closed: | Major Holidays | Address: | Exhibition Road, |
| Tube: | South Kensington | | South Kensington, |
| | (Piccadilly, | | SW7 2DD |
| | District Line) | Tel: | 071-938-8111 |

The museum is situated between the Geological
Museum and the Natural History Museum. It portrays
the rise and development of science, technology,
industry, and medicine, of scientific treasures and
pleasures via apparatus, and has demonstrations of all
kinds. That's the famous Foucault pendulum at the
entrance. The Sainsbury Gallery explains science's
impact on today's food, with hands-on displays, a food
pyramid, and a smellorama. The children's gallery on
the ground floor is vivid and fascinating. There's a

mock-up of a rocket launch pad and plenty of hands-on demos. The Wellcome Museum galleries on the upper floors have full-scale reconstructions of major events in medical history. Be sure to visit the Exploration of Space Gallery, and surely Gibson's Pharmacy. The Science Museum is one of London's major "discovered" tourist attractions.

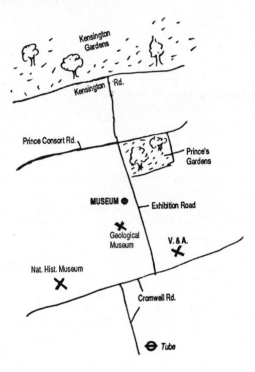

## SHAKESPEARE GLOBE MUSEUM

| | | | |
|---|---|---|---|
| **Open:** | Mon.-Sat. 10-5; Sun. 2-5 | **Type:** | Miscellaneous |
| **Closed:** | Major Holidays | **Address:** | Bear Gardens, Bankside, Southwark, SE1 9EB |
| **Tube:** | Cannon Street (Circle/District Line) | **Tel:** | 071-928-6342 |
| **Entry:** | £1.00 | | |

The museum, just a few yards away from the original site of Shakespeare's Globe Theatre, is housed in an 18th-century warehouse. The setting abounds with Shakespearean overtones and memorabilia. The museum traces the history of Elizabethan theater from the mid-1550s onward, through posters and drawings portraying Shakespearean characters as well as small replicas of Elizabethan and Jacobean playhouses. Plans for an entire new center include an authentic Elizabethan Globe Playhouse as it was in 1599, an exhibition of Elizabethan/Jacobean theater works, historical memorabilia, a gift shop, and a second theater that will accurately duplicate Inigo Jones' architectural design. Planners hope the center will be completed by 1992. Stroll through the neighborhood. It's called Southwark and represents London's current effort to streamline the south side of the Thames. It is succeeding.

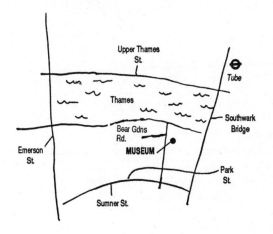

## SIR JOHN SOANE'S MUSEUM

| | | | |
|---|---|---|---|
| **Open:** | Tues.-Sat. 10-5 | **Entry:** | Free |
| **Closed:** | Sun., Mon., | **Type:** | Individual |
| | Major Holidays, | **Address:** | 13 Lincoln's Inn |
| | month of August | | Fields, WC2A |
| **Tube:** | Holborn | | 3BP |
| | (Piccadilly, | **Tel:** | 071-405-2107 |
| | Central Line) | | |

Upon entering, I suggest you buy the small catalog at the bookshop because this is, without doubt, one of the most complicated museums in London, the home of John Soane, eminent architect and extravagant collector. It was he who designed these odd premises. Through clever use of mirrors, level changes, unusual lighting, room division, and altered proportions, he created an illusion that is, to say the least, intriguing. It would be impossible to properly describe the design, configuration, conformity, and relation of one room to another or the contents that cram each salon from floor to ceiling, comprising a curious collection of paintings, drawings, sculpture, and other works of art. That is Sir John at age 75, done by Lawrence, hanging on the dining room wall. There are about 18 buildings in or near London attributable to Sir John Soane, including the Bank of England, the Royal Hospital in Chelsea, and the Dulwich Picture Gallery.

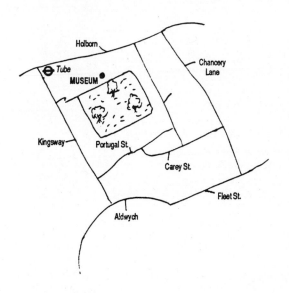

## STATE APARTMENTS (Kensington Palace)

| | | | |
|---|---|---|---|
| **Open:** | Mon.-Sat. 9-5; Sun. 1-5 | **Entry:** | £1.50 |
| **Closed:** | Major Holidays | **Type:** | General |
| **Tube:** | High St., Kensington (Circle/District Line) | **Address:** | Kensington Palace, W8 4PX |
| | | **Tel:** | 071-937-9561 |

The best part about visiting royal palaces is that you gain insight into the private side of that otherwise separate and isolated world of royalty. These elegant apartments were designed by Sir Christopher Wren in 1680. The first occupants were William and Mary in 1689, although most of the existing furnishings date from Queen Victoria's reign, about the 1850s, and several of her arrangements are intact. The private collections of portraits and paintings of monarchs, unfortunately unidentified, hang on lush wood-paneled walls. Decorative arts fill the apartments. Once outside, allow a few moments pause at the Edwardian sunken garden/pool. Then, it's a few steps away to the Round Pond for a model boat race (weekends only). Perhaps you might even rent a lounge (wood and canvas beach chair) and watch the world go by, a favorite pastime many Londoners indulge in on one of those rare sunny days.

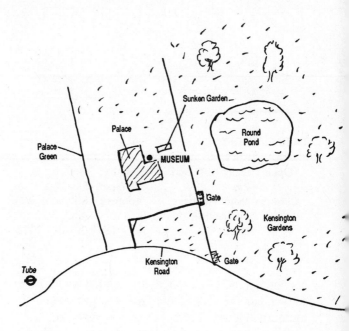

## TATE GALLERY

| | | | |
|---|---|---|---|
| **Open:** | Daily 10-6; Sun. 2-6 | **Entry:** | Free |
| **Closed:** | Major Holidays | **Type:** | Fine Arts |
| **Tube:** | Pimlico (Victoria Line) | **Address:** | Millbank, SW1P 4RG |
| | | **Tel:** | 071-821-1313 |

It's not that the Tate is large. It's just that what's there is so fine. For sheer elegance, Tate is a must on your museum itinerary. The building, 100 years old, is a superb example of neo-classical architecture. The Gallery devotes itself primarily to two themes—British artists, particularly Turner, Blake, and the Pre-Raphaelites, and modern paintings. The Sculpture Gallery at the entrance will win your heart not only for its statuary but also for its simple grandeur, comparable to Michelangelo's Laurentian Library in Florence. The

Clore Gallery, added in 1987, contains Turner's works solely, giving the Tate the unique honor of possessing the world's largest collection of works by one artist. One rare treat is a Turner self-portrait dated 1800. Under new directorship, Tate has undergone major refurbishing and has never looked so well. And there are two equally fine gift shops—one in the main building, the other in the Clore.

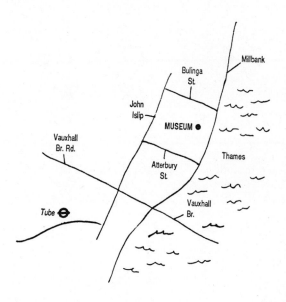

## THEATRE MUSEUM

| | | | |
|---|---|---|---|
| **Open:** | Tues.-Sun. 11-7 | **Type:** | Miscellaneous |
| **Closed:** | Mondays | **Address:** | 1E Tavistock St., |
| **Tube:** | Covent Garden | | WC2E 7PA |
| **Entry:** | £2.00 | **Tel:** | 071-836-7891 |

This museum is a kind of wonderland with an illusion of innocence. Galleries show the history and development of the British stage from Shakespeare's time until today, through drawings, prints, photographs, musical scores, costumes, playbills, theatrical memorabilia, and scenes from plays. Recorded dialogue from stage performances by Sir John Gielgud, Sir Lawrence Olivier, Sir Richard Burton, Dame Edith Evans, Dame Wendy Hiller, and other memorable theater artists is spoken through loud-speakers. Two galleries feature changing exhibitions relating to theater arts. The velvet-lined picture gallery downstairs is available for private receptions. It's next to the small theater where visiting groups perform. The tea room remains open till 8 p.m. for pre-curtain light dinner. Tickets for London's neighboring theaters are sold here. After your visit, Covent Garden and its environs entice you to a perfect stroll.

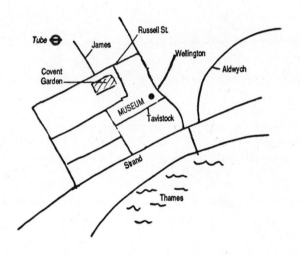

## TOWER BRIDGE MUSEUM

| | | | |
|---|---|---|---|
| **Open:** | Daily 10-6 | **Entry:** | £1.00 |
| **Closed:** | Major Holidays | **Type:** | General |
| **Tube:** | Tower Hill | **Address:** | Tower Bridge, |
| | (Circle/District | | SE1 2UP |
| | Line) | **Tel:** | 071-407-0922 |

Tower Bridge, one of the world's most renowned
bridges, is a unique symbol of Victorian engineering
and architecture. This visit is divided into two seg-
ments. The first takes you to the North Tower of the
Bridge. Take the elevator to the third level for an
historic overview of the Bridge through drawings,
paintings, and memorabilia showing the design,
function, and operation of all previous bridges across
the Thames since Roman times. Climb to another level
for a panoramic view of London as you cross a covered

walkway to the South Tower. Descend to the engine rooms, which are the second segment of the museum. Here are the original steam engines and boilers that powered the bridge's raising and lowering. Of course, you know there's an exact duplicate of Tower Bridge located in Lake Havasu, Arizona. The Design Museum is nearby. Follow the signs.

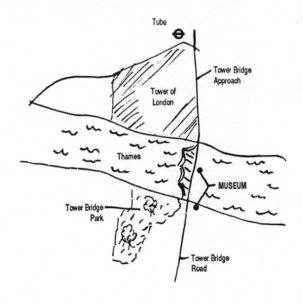

## VICTORIA & ALBERT MUSEUM

| | | | |
|---|---|---|---|
| **Open:** | Mon.-Sat. 10-6; Sun. 2:30-6 | **Entry:** | Free |
| | | **Type:** | Fine Arts |
| **Closed:** | Major Holidays | **Address:** | South |
| **Tube:** | South Kensington (Piccadilly, District Line) | | Kensington, SW7 2RL |
| | | **Tel:** | 071-938-8500 |

The Victoria & Albert, also known as the V&A, portrays itself as a museum of ornamental art, applied arts, and design. It is, in fact, committed to design from all ages, styles, and countries in addition to its unexcelled collection of sculptures, watercolors, portrait miniatures, and photography. As is the case with all London's museums, the V&A has its own unique personality. The collections within are so ambitious and exciting that it is difficult to imagine how any museum could approach it. Do not attempt the V&A in one day. I suggest that you confine yourself to those exhibitions you prefer, unless you have the luxury of several days' time. The museum has recently undergone major renovation, much to its advantage. Two exhibits not to be missed are the Jewel Rooms and the Raphael Cartoons. Keep your eye on your watch, though. Amidst all this radiant exuberance time flies, and the closing hours may catch you unaware.

## WALLACE COLLECTION

| | | | |
|---|---|---|---|
| **Open:** | Daily 10-5; Sun. 2-5 | **Type:** | Fine Arts |
| **Closed:** | Major Holidays | **Address:** | Hertford House, Manchester Square, W1M 6BN |
| **Tube:** | Bond Street (Jubilee Line) | | |
| **Entry:** | Free | **Tel:** | 071-935-0687 |

The Hertford Mansion, built in the late 1700s for the wealthy Wallace family and beautifully restored recently, is a splendorous collection begun more than 100 years ago by Mrs. Richard Wallace. The museum's collection consists of superb works handed down through generations of fastidious Wallace collectors. It consists not only of prized master paintings but sculpture, decorative arts, and porcelains of the highest order. The entire contents of the mansion are intact at all times; that is, no works of art may be added to or borrowed from the collection. The European and Oriental arms and armor collection dates back to the 14th century and is one of the most magnificent in the world. Oddly enough, it's one of the very few of its kind in London. My favorite piece in this museum is Franz Hals' "The Laughing Cavalier." The Wallace, one of the world's most distinguished private collections, is precisely what high-caliber art should be—perfection.

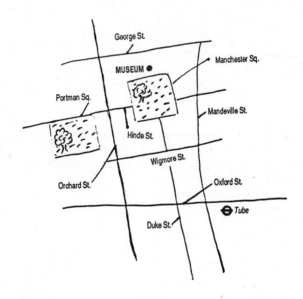

## WESTMINSTER ABBEY MUSEUM

| | | | |
|---|---|---|---|
| **Open:** | Daily 10:30-4 | **Type:** | Religious |
| **Closed:** | Major Holidays | **Address:** | Westminster |
| **Tube:** | Westminster | | Abbey, SW1P |
| | (Circle/District | | 3PA |
| | Line) | **Tel:** | 071-222-5152 |
| **Entry:** | £1.00 | | |

There are three separate chambers below the Abbey, and although only one of the three is called a museum, we shall treat all three as one. One ticket allows entry to all three rooms. The first is the large octagonal Chapter House, used by Benedictine monks in the 12th century. It's of beautiful artistry with a medieval tiled floor, sculptures, wall paintings, and six monumental stained glass windows. The second, the 11th-century vaulted Pyx Chamber, was used as the Abbey's Sacristy and gold and silver treasury. Its precious chalices, flagons, bowls, and dishes are still here. The third room is the Undercroft Museum, a vaulted chamber, built during the 11th century and converted into a museum in 1987. It holds the Abbey's collections of royal effigies, or death masks, begun in the 1300s, replicas of jeweled coronation regalia, 12th-century sculptures, and 13th-century glass panels. There is a sensitive side to history presented here. It's difficult to believe these generations of royalty lived, flourished, and died 700 years ago.

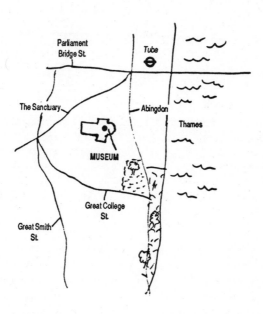

## WILLIAM MORRIS GALLERY

| | | | |
|---|---|---|---|
| **Open:** | Tues.-Sat. 10-1, 2-5 | **Entry:** | Free |
| **Closed:** | Sun., Mon., Major Holidays | **Type:** | Decorative Arts |
| | | **Address:** | Lloyd Park, Forest Road, E17 4PP |
| **Tube:** | Walthamstow (Victoria Line) | **Tel:** | 081-527-5544 |

This was the residence of the Morris family for several years. William Morris was fascinating. Not only was he a designer of books, furnishings, homes, textiles, and wallpaper but he was a weaver, a distinguished artist, a writer, a student of architecture, a printmaker, political spokesman of the Socialist Party, and founder of the Arts & Crafts movement in England. His intellectuality and love for Gothic principles and philosophy dominate his distinct style of ornamentation. Morris' esoteric colleagues were of equal talent and intelligence. Some of their creative genius decorates the museum with paintings and decorative arts. Morris suffered from melancholia, and photographs of him, circled by his family and friends, reflect this unhappiness. Morris is regarded as one of England's most versatile and innovative creators of the decorative arts. His unique style of design still enjoys unsurpassed popularity. There's a collection of Pre-Raphaelite paintings upstairs.

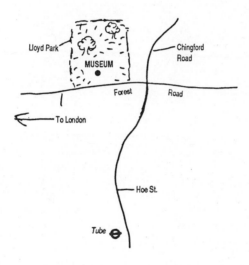

## WIMBLEDON LAWN TENNIS MUSEUM

| | | | |
|---|---|---|---|
| **Open:** | Tues.-Sat. 11-5; Sun. 2-5 | **Entry:** | £1.00 |
| | | **Type:** | Miscellaneous |
| **Closed:** | Mon., Holidays, Wimbledon Championship | **Address:** | The All England Club, Church Road, SW19 5AE |
| **Tube:** | Southfields (District Line) | **Tel:** | 081-946-6131 |

The museum is contained in a building adjoining the famous Centre Court. Look down into the Court from the terrace of the museum. Lawn tennis history is portrayed in chronological order from early Grecian days as a polite pastime onward, and the first championship tournament was held in 1877. You will see lawn tennis as played by the Victorians, the Edwardians, and the stars of the forties, fifties, sixties, and on up to current times. Changing fashion in dress and equipment, trophies through the years, and a racquet-maker's workshop are presented in galleries that demonstrate lawn tennis' social background. Displays are accompanied by listening points describing all exhibits and tennis protocol and parameters. Of course, the infamous rubber ball is given its just due and proper place in history. A small audio-visual theater demonstrates the game of tennis. You'll enjoy the museum shop too; the gifts are smashing.

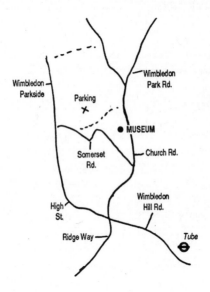

# INDEX BY CATEGORY

## RELIGIOUS

## SCIENCE

London Eye     0870·5000600